MAURITIUS

FROM THE AIR

Pages 6-7: *Near Mahébourg on the east coast,*
the Ile aux Cerfs (Stag Island) is a fifteen-minute trip from the coast by speedboat.
Nowadays stags have been replaced by tourists on its white sandy beaches.
Pages 8-9: *At the south-western tip of the island,*
the Morne Brabant, its name reminiscent of the Dutch, is a basalt peak rising to 558 metres.
Runaway slaves once used to hide there. The landscape here is one of the strangest
and most beautiful in Mauritius; the sunsets are magnificent.
The lagoon surrounding the island is bordered by a barrier reef with two fairways:
the Passe de l'Ambulante, named after a ship that ran aground there in the eighteenth century,
and the Passe Saint-Jacques. On the right, Fourneau islet can be seen.
Pages 10-13: *Sugar cane, with its high resistance to cyclones,*
covers most of the arable land, croossed by roads and paths and dotted with mounds
of stones removed from the fields.

The photographer dedicates this book to Gisella, and would like to
express his thanks to pilots Rui Catarino and Tony Pirès of Air Mauritius Helicopters.

Translated from the French by Ann Frater

First published in South Africa in 1993 by
Southern Book Publishers. P.O. Box 3103, Halfway House,
1685, Republic of South Africa

ISBN 1-86812-455 X
Publisher's number: 106

Colour separation by Far East Offset, Kuala Lumpur
and Colourscan Co Pte Ltd, Singapore
Printed by Tien Wah Press Pte Ltd, Singapore

TEXT BY GENEVIEVE DORMANN
PHOTOGRAPHS BY GUIDO ALBERTO ROSSI

MAURITIUS

FROM THE AIR

SOUTHERN
BOOK PUBLISHERS

CONTENTS

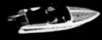

*P*ort Louis is situated in an amphitheatre of mountains. On the right is the Vallée des Prêtres. On the left is the Montagne des Signaux from which lookouts used to announce the arrival of ships. Today they have been replaced by radar. On the extreme left the Montagne du Pouce can be seen.

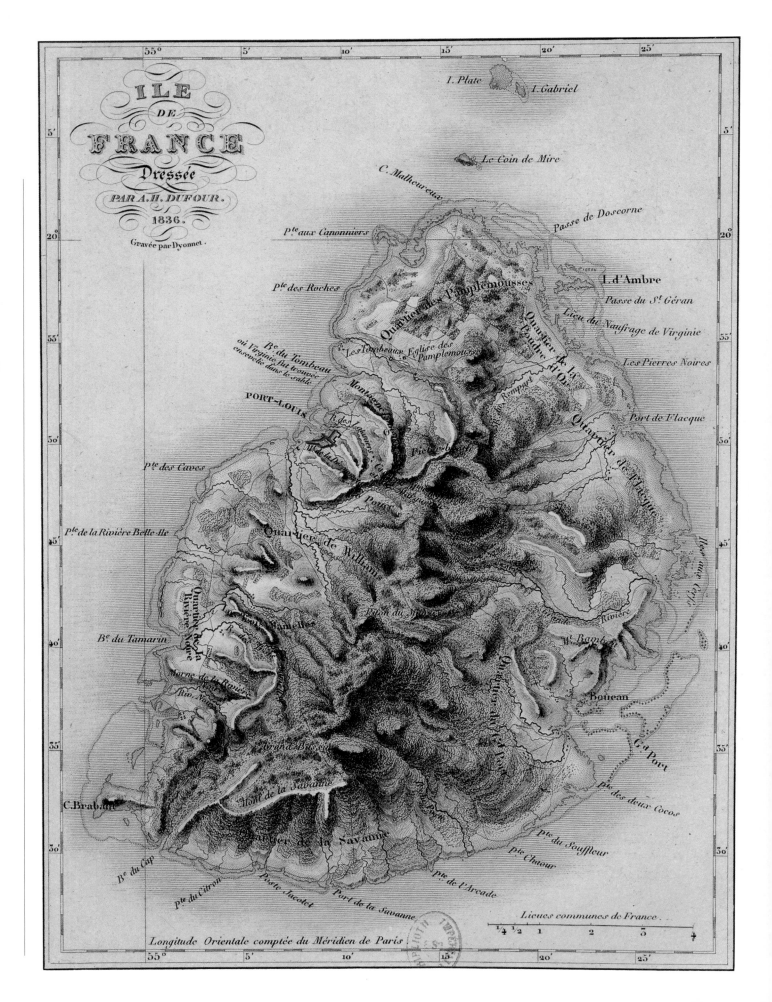

*T*his map engraved in 1836 gives a good view of the varied terrain of the island. It commemorates the fiftieth anniversary of the novel *Paul et Virginie* (1788), mentioning the spot where the Saint-Géran was shipwrecked and the place on the opposite coast where the unfortunate Virginie is said to have been found buried in the sand at the Baie du Tombeau.

FROM ISLE DE FRANCE TO MAURITIUS ISLAND

S ituated on the twentieth parallel, to the north of the Tropic of Capricorn, between the continents of Africa and India, and 160 kilometres to the east of Réunion Island, the 1,872 square kilometres of the island of Mauritius represent a tiny dot in the Indian Ocean. Like the neighbouring island of Réunion, Mauritius is volcanic in origin, but it is much older: it is 70 million years old. Its volcanoes ceased to be active well over a million years ago, and its craters are extinct.

The oval-shaped island rises from the coast up to a central plateau about 500 metres in altitude at its highest point. This plateau is encircled by three mountain ranges: the Montagne Longue range in the north-east; the Rivière Noire and Savanne chains in the west and south-west, and the Montagnes Bambous in the south-east. A practically unbroken circle of coral reefs surrounds the island, protecting it from sharks and creating a striking lagoon. The shore, alternating between white sand and black rocks similar to the Breton coastline, forms natural havens. One of the charms of this tropical island is the diversity of its landscape: sometimes reminiscent of the Jura mountains, sometimes of Scotland and even, in certain spots, of the Beauce region of France, but with sugar cane instead of corn.

The Mauritian climate is, for Europeans, an eternal summer: warm from November to April (30°C maximum), with cyclones of varying force from January to March, sometimes torrential but brief rainfalls from January to May and a cool season from May to October. One surprising feature of the climate is that the weather may be cold and rainy on the heights of Curepipe, while 25 kilometres away the sun's heat is harsh on the west coast and Port Louis is stifling. This explains the variety of the vegetation: grass and vegetables on the plateau, forests and dry plants on the coast. And everywhere are the brilliant colours of flowers, the vermilion of coral trees, the pinks and purples of bougainvillaea, the vivid yellows of cassia and allamanda. Everywhere, too, is sugar cane.

The island was first indicated by Arab navigators on their sea-charts between the seventh and tenth centuries, under the name of "Dina Arobi". But they did not stop there. At the beginning of the sixteenth century the Portuguese arrived. In 1511 Domingo Fernandez anchored his caravel, the *Santa Maria di Serra*, just long enough to take on fresh water and change the name Dina Arobi to "Ilha do Cirné" - "Isle of the Swan" - perhaps on account of a large, strange bird, the dodo, which was waddling about there. Another Portuguese, Pero Mascarenhas, gave his name to the three islands still known as the Mascarene Islands: Réunion, the largest, Mauritius and Rodrigues, the smallest.

After the Portuguese, more than eighty years went by without any further visitors to the island. Then, on 17 September 1598, five Dutch ships sailing towards India under the orders of Commander Van Warwyck stopped in one of the two bays of the island suitable for mooring: the south-east bay, now known as the Baie du Grand Port. Warwyck gave the bay his name and changed the name of the island from "Cirné" to "Mauritius" in honour of Maurice of Nassau, Prince of the Netherlands. But this episode was still only a call in port to take possession. During the years that followed other Dutch convoys put into Warwyck Bay. On 1 January 1606, the Dutch tried out the other natural harbour situated at the north-east of the island (now Port Louis). Here, under the lee, weighing was easier than at Warwyck Bay, where the south-east tradewind blew. The shore was covered with enormous tortoises for which reason they named this hospitable harbour the Bay of Tortoises.

A few years later, Pieter Both, first governor of the Dutch Indies, was shipwrecked not far from this spot, along with a large cargo of spices, silks, indigo, diamonds and Chinese porcelain from Indonesia. Caught in a cyclone, Both tried to take shelter in the Bay of Tortoises and lost his life on one of the two ships, the *Banda*, washed onto the reefs off the coast of Médine. Today, one of the most impressive mountains of Mauritius bears his name.

Four centuries later, a secret map drawn up by the Dutch of that period was discovered in the Bibliothèque Nationale in Paris, enabling the wreck of the *Banda* to be located. Finally it was found, and chests of porcelain from the Ming Era were raised from the bottom of the sea. They had been preserved intact, held fast in the silt under the *Banda*'s cannon.*

But the eighteenth-century Dutch were not the only ones interested in Mauritius. Although the large island of Madagascar was the main attraction for European seafarers, the English, Danes and French began to take an interest in the still-deserted island of Mauritius, covered with forests, a resting place on the route to India. They landed and went on their way again, but this did not suit the Dutch, who decided to move in seriously and set up a colony. In May 1638 a contingent from Holland landed in the south-east port, chosen in preference to the north harbour where Pieter Both was shipwrecked.

An eighteenth-century traveller described Mauritius as a verdant island whose ebony trees supplied the most beautiful wood in the entire Orient, with coastal waters abounding in fish and tortoises so big that "four sailors having mounted on the back of one of them, it nevertheless walked as easily as if it had not been laden". He described a multitude of birds, so little threatened that one could take them with one's hand, numerous heron and the famous dodo "with neither wings nor tail, whose flesh is so tough that no heat can cook it".**

The occupation of Mauritius by the Dutch lasted only twenty-odd years. They used the island simply for commercial purposes: the slave trade with Madagascar and intensive export of ebony. Ecology was not their main concern. They ravaged the forests and the over-trusting birds of Mauritius, killing the turtle doves with sticks and exterminating for-ever the poor dodos in spite of their inedible flesh. They called the dodo "Wolgwogel", meaning "bird of repulsion". Their only positive contribution was the introduction of oxen, sheep, pigs, poultry and, above all, deer and sugar cane imported from Java. In 1710, disheartened by cyclones and rats, the Dutch abandoned the island. They demolished the buildings erected at Flacq and Grand Port in the south-east, leaving behind only a few slaves who had taken refuge in the woods and survived by whatever means they could.

Five years later on 20 September 1715, Guillaume Dufresne d'Arsel officially took possession of the island in the name of the King of France. It was henceforth named the Isle de France. The north-east port became Port Louis, in honour of the young Louis XV and to remind the Breton settlers of Port Louis at Lorient. As for Warwyck Port, it became Port Bourbon.

In April 1722, after ten months at sea, the *Diane* and the *Athalante*, vessels of the Compagnie des Indes, administrator of the new French possession, put ashore on the Isle de France. They were carrying the first governor, Denis Denyon, and the first settlers from France, or at least those who had survived scurvy, storms and the pirates swarming on the coasts of Africa and India. The long and terrible voyage had claimed many victims.

At Groix the two ships took on board a Swiss company of 210 men, soldiers, stewards, officers and officials; twenty women and about thirty children. Almost half never reached

* Dumas, Jacques, *Fortune de
Mer à l'île Maurice*, Atlas Films

** Le Cene, Michel-Charles
(bookseller), *Voyages Célèbres et
Remarquables du Seigneur Jean
Albert de Mandelsco*, Amsterdam
MDCXXVII

the Isle de France. The survivors had not seen the last of their troubles. Not only did they have to erect shelters as soon as they landed, since the island had no buildings apart from the ruins of the south-east port left by the Dutch, but they also had to contend with heat, cyclones, rats, food scarcity and the extortions of fugitive Negro slaves who looted, killed and sowed terror. The three governors who succeeded Denyon failed to improve their situation. The settlers had to await the arrival of La Bourdonnais in 1735 before life became less hellish.

Bertrand Mahé de La Bourdonnais was only thirty-six years old when he landed at the Isle de France, but he already had an eventful career behind him. Born at Saint-Malo, he had been sailing in the merchant navy since the age of ten. At twenty he became a mate with the Compagnie des Indes. He made money at Pondicherry, hunted pirates on the coast of Malabar, and commanded a vessel of the Portuguese navy. Appointed governor of the Isle de France and Bourbon (Réunion), he arrived at Port Louis on 4 June 1735. It is to this brilliant man that the Port Louis and Mauritius we know today owe their first structural organisation.

Both sailor and merchant, La Bourdonnais quickly understood the potential importance of this French pebble on the India route, provided it were made into a well-planned port on the model of his native Saint-Malo. It could become a commercial depot, a haven for privateers and a port where vessels, often arriving greatly damaged by the long voyage, could call for repairs. This demanded well-organised guilds and a settled colony composed of people more useful than adventurers and transient good-for-nothings. Within five years he had succeeded in instilling order where, previously, anarchy had reigned. Buildings of primary necessity were constructed - a hospital for the sick, revictualling warehouses and a bakery. La Bourdonnais organised and fortified the port and had a fairway and dry dock built. Later he began to build dinghies, long-boats and, finally, rated ships.

But this sailor and soldier was also a town-planner. He began by satisfying the most urgent need - water - by digging a canal to convey the water of the Grande Rivière to the port. Bricks and lime were manufactured so that the wooden huts could be replaced by real buildings capable of resisting cyclones. Houses, shops and offices appeared. Roads were laid towards Pamplemousses and Moka, on which waggons were drawn by oxen imported from Madagascar. To reduce the food shortage, he encouraged the settlers to cultivate the land. He had sugar cane planted and was responsible for the first sugar refineries established at Port-Sud and Pamplemousses. He also introduced cassava to the island. For his private use, La Bourdonnais built a manor-house at Pamplemousses on the estate of Monplaisir.

All that remained to be done was to create a settled society, for which the founding of families had to be encouraged. But women were in short supply. "The Company, realising this, had a certain number [of women] brought to the Isle de France in the beginning. Some of these, from the communities of Nantes and Saint-Malo, had been raised 'in virtue and work'. But they were the exception. Most were recruited in much less respectable circles."* La Bourdonnais brought over from Bourbon young girls who were likely to become peace-able wives and ensure stable homes. He also imported fencing, dancing and music masters to supply the colony with amusements. In later years Port Louis was to be filled with the strains of oboes and violins.

* Toussaint, Auguste, *Port Louis de l'île Maurice*, Presses Universitaires de France

In 1803 General Decaen was named governor of the Isle de France and Port Louis became Port Napoléon. This engraving of the Isle de France by J. Milbert shows the town of Port Napoléon from the Montagne du Pouce.

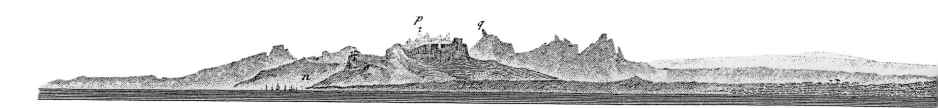

La Bourdonnais certainly earned his statue, which still looks out to sea at the end of the Place d'Armes. A replica of this statue was erected on the ramparts of Saint-Malo in 1989, belated justice to a man who was exposed to the jealousy of his predecessor Cossigny, and who spent two undeserved years in the Bastille prison on his return to France in 1746, due to the ingratitude of his contemporaries.

In 1767, when the Compagnie des Indes went bankrupt, Bourbon and the Isle de France came under the government of the king, and new administrators arrived at Port Louis. One of the most effective, Pierre Poivre, pledged to rob the Dutch of their monopoly of the spice trade.

On 27 July 1770, the *Vigilant* and the *Etoile du Matin* landed at Port Louis from the Moluccas with a cargo of nutmeg and clove seedlings. The planting of these was to give less successful results in the Isle de France than at Bourbon, but Poivre remained undaunted. He sent out botanical missions to every part of the world. From China came cuttings of tea, rice and indigo; from Africa, the Americas and Tahiti arrived fruit trees: jujubes, lemons and peaches. Lychees, mangoes and guavas started to grow. He imported new trees, either useful or decorative, and many of those marvellous flowers that still delight the eye on Mauritius. Within five years, Pierre Poivre had begun to transform the garden of Pamplemousses into one of the most beautiful in the world.

While the American War of Independence wreaked havoc in India, life was merry in the Isle de France, where the troops often called into port. So merry, indeed, that Pierre André de Suffren, the famous French naval captain, expressed anxiety in his journal: "This country is becoming soft; there are abundant pretty women and the way of life is very pleasant. Money is made by trading. All this is better than making war; thus one remains here as long as one can." So he proposed, in order to harden his troops, to "flee above all this island which is like the isle of Calypso". The prudish Bernardin de Saint-Pierre, who worked in the Isle de France for six years as an engineer, was for his part utterly shocked by the carefree and joyous life lead by the French at Port Louis and denounced them as "extremely insensitive to everything that delights honest souls".

The turmoil of the French Revolution reached Mauritius in a very attenuated form. A few hot-heads aped the French demonstrations and celebrations, some speeches were made, a colonial assembly was created and the royal symbols done away with; but there was no violence or carnage. For form's sake a guillotine was erected, but its only victim was a goat used to test the blade. Though they acquiesced in the abolition of the slave trade, the colon-ists were categorically opposed to emancipation without compensation.

The war with England which broke out in 1793 was of more concern to the little colony, particularly the privateering war in the Indian Ocean which brought fame to pirates such as Robert Surcouf, whose portrait and pistol are kept in the Mahébourg museum. From this era of piracy dates the legend - or reality - of considerable treasure buried on Mauritius.

In 1803 General Decaen was appointed governor of the Isle de France and of Bourbon, henceforth called Réunion. Port Louis became Port Napoléon. In 1810, the English took possession of Réunion and decided to seize Mauritius, an important strategic point in the Indian Ocean and, above all, a den of pirates who greatly endangered their ships. On 20 August, they attempted to land via the Baie du Grand Port in the south-east but, after a

*A*nother panoramic view of the Isle de France by J. Milbert. From left to right, Port Napoléon (n), Morne de la Découverte (o), the Pieter Both peak (p), the Montagne du Pouce (q), the Montagne des Trois Mamelles (r) and the Morne Brabant.

desperate naval battle, they retreated, losing five ships. The Battle of Grand Port was the only naval battle won against the English during Napoléon's reign and merited, as such, an inscription under the Arc de Triomphe in Paris. This French victory was, however, only a reprieve, for three months later the English attacked in force from the north of the island and marched victoriously on Port Louis.

What could Decaen do against ten thousand men, with a defence of only about two thousand regular soldiers? To avoid a massacre he chose to capitulate, but on condition that the French land and sea troops might leave without difficulty and that the island's inhabitants could keep their property, religion, language and customs, and had the right to leave the island with their possessions, if they so wished, within the next two years. The English Commander Abercromby accepted these conditions, pleased with such a cheap solution and in haste to occupy the place.

From now on, the island was no longer the Isle de France. It regained its old Dutch name of Mauritius, which it kept even after independence in 1968.

In the 1814 peace treaty with France, the English gave back Réunion to the French but kept Mauritius, being interested in the port. Today, Mauritians of French origin are a minority. But respect for the conditions of capitulation demanded by Decaen, together with the fact that there were never many English settlers on Mauritius (emigrants from England preferred India, South Africa or Australia) explains why, nearly two centuries later, French cultural influence remains very strong. Even though cars are driven on the left and English is the official language, most of the names of towns and villages - Mahébourg, Souillac, Port Louis and Poudre d'Or - preserve the memory of the first inhabitants. On a day at the races in Port Louis the municipal band plays the old French song "Ah! vous dirais-je, maman", while all Mauritians, whether of Indian, Chinese or Madagascan origin, speak French and especially Creole, a sort of national language forming a link between the different ethnic groups. This language is a living, poetic dialect through which the music of old French words can still be detected.

Throughout the nineteenth century, Great Britain, new master of the island, continued the work initiated by France on Mauritius: road-building, town-planning, the construction of two railway lines (as early as 1864), the creation of banks and the development of sugar-cane cultivation.

In 1816 a terrible fire destroyed a fifth of Port Louis. Farquhar, the governor, prohibited wooden walls, attics and roofs as they were too vulnerable to fire and hurricanes. A new Port Louis rose out of the ruins: a city with wider streets, this time well-ordered and perfectly straight, and fine stone-built houses, some of which are still in existence near the rue Saint-Georges. From June to October the social season was in full swing in the renovated town. The port was full of ships, coming and going with cargo and news from all over the world. Festivals, concerts, balls, theatres and horse-races were thronged with people.

However, Port Louis hardly smelled pleasant. Canalisation was still non-existent, water was scarce and all-purpose sewers were unheard of. With its dense population and stifling climate, it was favourable ground for epidemics caused by the deadly germs brought in by the ships. After smallpox in the eighteenth century came rabies in 1813, then cholera from the Philippines in 1819. People began to flee the town. Another cholera epidemic in 1854 drove

These subsequently coloured photographs of Port Louis are the work of a traveller of noble lineage, Frederick Fiebig, who voyaged in the Indian Ocean around 1850 and stopped at Mauritius before ending his journey at the Cape. Port Louis (above) already reveals considerable activity, judging by the lines of ships at anchor in the harbour. This rather angular urban development is offset by large areas of vegetation and the surrounding hills.

ten thousand inhabitants from Port Louis and Pamplemousses to the inland region where the climate was cooler and healthier. The terrible malaria epidemic that raged from 1861 to 1867 was the main cause of the decline of Port Louis. This decline benefited the Wilhems Plains area where villages, and then towns, sprung up: Beau Bassin, Rose-Hill, Quatre Bornes, Vacoas, Moka, and above all Curepipe, which in time became a kind of second capital. But Port Louis remained the business and trade centre.

It was also during the British colonial period that immigration from India reached its peak. Slavery was abolished in 1835, but the expansion of sugar-cane cultivation required an increase in labour. Slaves were replaced by "volunteers". The "coolie trade", a sort of slave traffic in disguise but officially allowed, introduced a large number of Indians from Madras, Calcutta and Bombay up until 1809. In 1895 the total population of Mauritius was 371,000, a figure that included 256,000 Indians. Most of the Chinese arrived on the island at the end of the nineteenth century; they were to monopolise a large part of the retail trade. The term "Creole" covered three groups of people: whites of European stock, coloured people and emancipated slaves (about 42,000), more than half of whom were of African origin. The nineteenth-century Creoles comprised what is today known in Mauritius as the "general population", also including the large Indo-Mauritian and Sino-Mauritian groups.

The island's communications with the rest of the world were also developed under British colonial rule. In 1859 the first shipping line with Europe was established. A line link-ing England with Australia via Mauritius was opened in 1859 and, in 1864, the Messageries Impériales Françaises (Messageries Maritimes) connected Suez with Réunion, with an extension to Mauritius. Steam finally replaced sail at the end of the nineteenth century, and the harbour of Port Louis had to be reorganised to receive the new ships. At the beginning of the Second World War the Messageries Maritimes was suspended. Cut off from Réunion and Madagascar, Mauritius set up a naval and air base at Grand Port. An air-link was established with Diégo-Suarez and Johannesburg in 1944. This was the start of traffic at Plaisance Airport, where one arrives in Mauritius today.

On 12 March 1968, after 158 years of British colonisation, Mauritius became independent. It still remains a member of the Commonwealth, and its government is based on the British political system, with a prime minister and seventy members of parliament.

Today Mauritius is less than fifteen hours' flight from Paris or London. European and South African visitors arrive in ever-increasing numbers, convinced by the tourist agencies' praise of its white sandy beaches, its mountains, the luxurious mildness of its climate, the variations of the light, the hospitality of its inhabitants and the comfort of its hotels. But its charm lies in something quite different: in its French atmosphere - one of old France, which remarkably survives in spite of the ups and downs of the past. Even though Africa and Asia combine to ensure a colourful change of environment, and though the descendants of the early inhabitants are now only a very small minority, going to Mauritius is, especially for the French, taking a leap in time as well as a leap in space. The ghosts of La Bourdonnais and Surcouf, more in evidence than at Saint-Malo, welcome the visitor. There is something of Brittany in the wind swaying the fronds of the coconut palms, and the foam on the waves at the Pointe du Gris-Gris. Baudelaire walks in the Pamplemousses Garden and the young Paul-Jean Toulet is reunited with his Mauritian parents in the shade of Souillac.

*The Pieter Both
(800 metres), rising behind
Port Louis, is the highest peak
on Mauritius after the Piton,
near the Petite Rivière Noire.
It is a narrow cone of basalt
rock crowned by a curious
mushroom shape resembling
a human head. Scaling it is
considered an exploit and
several climbers have lost
their lives in the attempt.*

The population of Mauritius today is over one million, with a density of 526 inhabitants per square kilometre. Almost three quarters of the population are of Asian, Indian or Chinese origin. Of these, the Indo-Mauritians form 70% while the Sino-Mauritians represent 3%. The population of European and African origin accounts for 27%. Not more than about 4,000 people are descended from the first European settlers.

Port Louis, the capital, is situated in the north-east. As in the eighteenth century, it has the greatest population concentration, with 150,000 inhabitants today. It was under British rule that Port Louis acquired the cosmopolitan character it still possesses.

The town is both fascinating in all the historical memories it still preserves and exhausting because of its very hot climate and bustling everyday life: port activities, banking, a densely packed commercial centre, itinerant vendors, traffic jams (especially in the Chinese quarter around the Bazaar), the large central market for fruit, vegetables, spices and clothes. Many office workers and civil servants come to work here during the day but live outside Port Louis. In the evening the town quietens down and is completely transformed. The streets are emptied and the voices of the muezzins calling the faithful to prayer reverberate out to sea. On a hill stands Fort Adélaïde which was built between 1835 and 1840 by the British but never used. Today the fort is partly abandoned, serving only for theatrical or "sound and light" productions.

Neither La Bourdonnais, who laid its foundations in the seventeenth century, nor Conrad, who described nineteenth-century Port Louis in his novel *Chance*, would recognise today's enlarged and modernised port with its enormous warehouses. Yet, despite the spread of concrete which became rife in Mauritius in the 1960s, amid the multi-storey buildings, Port Louis has retained a few wooden houses dating from the beginnings of the town, a charming nineteenth-century theatre, churches, gardens - one of which sports a comical bust of Lenin - and some noble houses built before the exodus of the last century caused by epidemics. At the moment, a policy of intensive building is threatening the architectural heritage of Port Louis, and, sadly, beautiful old edifices are being demolished to be replaced with disproportionate blocks of flats.

Port Louis is also a very strange town, "one of the most occult places in the world", according to the Mauritian writer and painter Malcolm de Chazal. This opinion is con-fimed by the poet Robert Edward Hart (1891-1954), a native of Port Louis who witnessed extremely curious phenomena concerning haunted houses. With its mysteries, its pungent odours, its colours, deafening noises and immense ships riding at anchor, Port Louis is a curious blend of Africa and Asia. A town where time stands still, it remains one of the most attractive ports in the world.

Curepipe, with 55,000 inhabitants, is the third-largest urban centre after Beau Bassin/Rose-Hill and Port Louis, about twenty kilometres away. Situated at an altitude of 543 metres on the summit of the central plateau, it can be regarded as the "Swiss" town of Mauritius because of its climate, which is very cool in summer and rainy throughout the rest of the year (hence its vigorous vegetation). Created in the nineteenth century after the exodus from Port Louis due to malaria, Curepipe was for a long period the favourite residence of the European bourgeoisie. Though in the town centre little remains of the many attractive houses that have been ravaged by cyclones and replaced by ugly concrete

*T*his view
from the air shows the
installations of Port Louis,
a town whose activity
extends to the whole world:
fuel tanks, loading wharfs
for bulk sugar cane, and
the dry dock still known as
Trou Fanfaron, an echo
of the distant past.

blocks, on the outskirts (especially in the residential districts of Floréal, where the Soviet embassy is located, or Forest Side), there are numerous beautiful residences set in superb gardens enclosed by bamboo hedges. Diplomats often live in this area.

Although people of European extraction are a minority on Mauritius, Curepipe is still a "white" town in spirit, and the most European institutions on the island are found there: churches, Catholic schools, the Carnegie Library, the French Cultural Centre. Under the arcades, sheltered from the rain, is a big shopping centre. Imported products are found at the main supermarket, the Saturday haunt of middle-class housewives. With abundant quantities of fruit and vegetables at the central market, fashion boutiques and material shops, chemists, banks and restaurants, Curepipe is the town for "shopping where it's cool". The "in" thing is to live there during the week and go down to the coast for the weekend.

The two towns of Beau Bassin and Rose-Hill in the Wilhems Plains were merged into a single urban centre in 1896. Today there are 90,000 inhabitants, governed by one municipal council which sits at Rose-Hill. At an altitude of 300 metres, the climate is more temperate than on the coast and less rainy than at Curepipe.

Beau Bassin/Rose-Hill also developed in the nineteenth century. Since 1868 Rose-Hill has been the favourite town of the ethnic middle classes. Beau Bassin has some fine build-ings including the Tour Blanche and the Réduit adjacent to the Belfour Garden with its beautiful tropical trees. There are numerous religious establishments in these twin towns (Catholic and Anglican churches, mosques and Tamil temples) as well as educational insti-tutions (including five colleges), and important cultural activities. The Rose-Hill Theatre, built in 1930 and designed by the architect Mazérieux, has now dethroned that of Port Louis.

Quatre Bornes, near Rose-Hill, is the up-and-coming residential town. At 329 metres' altitude on the central plateau, at the foot of the Montagne du Corps de Garde, it enjoys a very pleasant climate with its many gardens and market-gardening farms. A few beautiful houses still exist behind the concrete frontage of the town centre. With its 55,000 inhab-itants, the town is expanding commercially and starting to rival Curepipe.

Merged under the same local government, the two urban centres of Vacoas and Phoenix have a population of 50,000. Vacoas with all its greenery is the most English town on the island. The British held a garrison there until 1968.

Created by Decaen in 1806, Mahébourg was for a long time the most important town in Mauritius after Port Louis. Situated in the south-east, near the Baie du Grand Port, this residential and military town was a centre of intense social life under the French of the Empire and at the start of the English colonisation. Deserted by its inhabitants during the epidemics, today it has a population of less than 20,000, consisting mainly of Indians and Chinese. There are numerous boutiques selling material, saris and Indian silks and there is an interesting naval museum in a beautiful Saint-Malo-style house surrounded by a large garden. It was here that the two wounded admirals, English and French, were nursed in the same room after commanding the two enemy fleets in the Battle of Grand Port.

Tourists are rare in this quiet, endearing little town where the houses are said to be even more haunted than at Port Louis. There is a lively open-air market situated near the sea where the fishermen dry their fish. Pierre Benoît's novel *Jamrose* is set in Mahébourg at the time of the Battle of Grand Port, a time which is easy to recreate in Mahébourg today.

Teeming with life, Port Louis today is the fascinating capital of Mauritius. With its old harbour, which Mahé de La Bourdonnais wanted to turn into a replica of the one at his native Saint-Malo, it was once the pirates' den of the Indian Ocean. Nowadays it is a centre for business and commerce. In the background, the Champ de Mars, originally a military parade-ground, became a much-frequented race-course during the British colonial period.

*S*hips from all around
the world anchor in the bay of Port Louis. In the
background, to the right, are the sugar warehouses,
and to the left is the vast Western Cemetery where
many pirates with French names are buried. Above:
ships anchored at the foot of the statue of
La Bourdonnais on the Place des Armes in front
of Parliament House.

The docks and warehouses at Trou Fanfaron were named after Nicolas Huet from Saint-Malo, known as "le Fanfaron" (the braggart), first licensee of the old dry dock designed by Tromelin. In 1781 the dock could hold six men-of-war and numerous other vessels.

*C*argo being shipped for Marseilles.
*Mauritius' main export is sugar, the product of its monoculture. The island
has to import flour, rice, meat, dairy products and general provisions. South
Africa, Australia and New Zealand are her most important trading partners.
Container ships from around the world moor at Port Louis.*

In the name of development and profit-making, concrete has covered Mauritius, gradually erasing the harmonious early structures. However young Mauritian architects are trying to limit unwarranted demolition and check this "Singaporisation" in order to preserve here, as in Réunion, an architectural heritage.

At the end of a path planted with imposing royal palms is Parliament House, the ground floor of which dates from the time of La Bourdonnais. The roof of this building was the first metal construction on the island. At the entrance is a statue of Queen Victoria which in summer is framed by the flowers of flame trees.

*T*he Town Hall of Curepipe is
a fine example of nineteenth-century Mauritian
architecture (centre-left of photo). It is awaiting
uncertain restoration. Nearby, the strange modern
market (above and following pages) where
commerce, with its tropical colours and smells, keeps
alive links with the past.

*V*acoas, *still popular with the British,*
was formerly the site of the headquarters of Her Majesty's civil servants. In the
foreground is the officers' mess, situated next to the golf course and the club
house, in fitting colonial style.

*T*he bandstand
in the botanical gardens
of Curepipe. Planted with
camphor trees, these gardens
are much frequented by
nannies and their charges
in the afternoons.

*W*ith its rare flowers and spices,
its lakes, tortoise pen and ancient sugar-cane mill, the Pamplemousses Garden
is amongst the most beautiful in the world. It was created in 1767 by Pierre
Poivre, who brought in species from every part of the world – rice from Cochin
China, nutmeg and clove trees from Manila, tea, camphor and much more. At
the end of the century the garden was taken in hand by Nicolas Céré, who
added trees and arbours, flowers and fruit. Today these ten acres are a delight
for botanists as well as amateur garden-lovers.

*T*he lake of
giant water lilies (Victoria
Amazonica), known more
prosaically to Mauritians
as "flan tins". Along these
banks strolled Mahé de
La Bourdonnais, Baudelaire,
Pierre Poivre ...

*T*he sprawling urban district including
Curepipe, Floréal, Vacoas and Phoenix contains a wide variety of housing
which reflects the diverse living conditions of the multiracial community,
from these bungalows, modest in spite of their gay colours ...

... To these villas, ensconced in their carefully trained vegetation and exuding ease and comfort, which could be set in the English countryside just as easily as in the tropics.

*A*t Vacoas, neatly designed, almost austere houses carry on the tradition and comfort of English homes with their manicured lawns and strictly clipped hedges.

*A*lthough he does not live there,
the Guest House is the official residence of the prime minister. Built in 1870 on
stone foundations, its central tower was added in 1904. The influence of the
English can be seen in the verandah, partly enclosed to form a bow window.
On the roof, next to one of the chimneys (a rare sight in Mauritius),
there is a solar water-heater.

*T*he Trou aux
Cerfs (previous pages) at
Curepipe is the oldest crater
of one of Mauritius' extinct
volcanoes. The bottom
(about 100 metres down)
can be reached by steep
paths winding through
rich vegetation to
a small natural lake. On
the road the meteorological
station that forecasts the
arrival of cyclones can be
seen. The Vacoas golf course
(right), as peaceful and
green as an English one.
The strange shapes of the
Rempart and Trois Mamelles
mountains are seen on
the horizon.

*T*he superb Maurice Rault Stadium at
Moka was inaugurated on the occasion of the second Indian Ocean Games
in 1985. Athletics competitions are held here, as well as football matches that
draw passionate crowds trained in the sport since childhood.

*S*ituated *on the Wilhems Plains, Quatre Bornes (Four Milestones) was named after the boundaries of two estates in the eighteenth century. This urban area with 55,000 inhabitants has a pleasant climate and is beginning to rival Curepipe as a commercial centre. Above: the traditional coach journeys from town to town, through the no-less traditional fields of sugar cane.*

*T*he lofty spire of the
Montmartre church at Rose-Hill rises not far from
the imposing Town Hall (opposite), of which the
main body and wings house the council hall,
a library and a famous theatre.

*S*ituated on the Rivière La Chaux
near the bay of Grand Port, the delightful little town of Mahébourg is perhaps -
along with Port Louis - the spot which preserves the most reminders of the
Mauritius of yesterday. Founded under the French Empire by Governor
Decaen, it was a centre of society life in the early days of the British colony.
Despite encroaching concrete and tourism, the graceful ghosts
of the past are still here.

The church of Notre Dame des Anges and its cross (1849). Mahébourg is said to be the home of Mauritian magic, which is inspired by the voodoo of Madagascar. Decaen, the last French governor, named the town in honor of Mahé de La Bourdonnais.

Dominated by the imposing Montagne du Corps de Garde, Rose-Hill takes its name from the hues of the early dawn. The town, created in the nineteenth century, has a young working-class population. It was declared a village in 1868 and merged with Beau Bassin in 1895. Today Beau Bassin/Rose-Hill has the highest population density on the island after Port Louis.

*M*ouchoir
Rouge is a small islet off
Mahébourg. A solitary
house, situated on a
wooded island with a jetty:
this is the ultimate dream
of every city dweller.

The sometimes monotonous aspect of the plains planted with sugar cane is oddly relieved by these mounds, known as "Creole pyramids", made of stones laboriously torn from the earth and piled up through the ages.

Tourists preoccupied by seaside amusements miss a great deal if they fail to visit the inland part of Mauritius. Although the island is small (1,872 square kilometres) and its greatest length is no more than 68 kilometres, its extremely varied landscapes change at every turn of the road and prevent any possibility of claustrophobia.

The extreme north, devoid of relief with its flat expanses of sugar cane, is not the prettiest inland area of Mauritius, but the landscape becomes more interesting as one goes south on the west side and returns on the east. There are three chains of strangely shaped mountains, so jagged in places that the poet Malcolm de Chazal declared they had been carved by the hand of proto-historic man, as the object of a cult. For de Chazal, Mauritius was one of the few remaining peaks of the lost Lemurian continent joined to Patagonia. Streams and rivers abound. Waterfalls cascade down the mountains into lakes bordered with waterlilies on which, at dusk, bullfrogs join in a symphony.

The coastal plains (180 metres above sea-level) border a central plateau of which the summit, Curepipe, is at a height of 500 metres. On the plains, one finds Indian almond trees bearing delicious nuts, coconut-palms whose leaves defy the cyclones, banyans with long aerial roots, breadfruit and jackfruit trees. And much more.

Although the primeval forest no longer covers more than one fifth of the country - the ebony and rosewood were ravaged during the period of Dutch occupation - the high ground has been partly replanted with mahogany and camphor, conifers and Eucalyptus. The dampest forest areas abound with tree-ferns, lianas, giant bamboos and the elegant ravenala palm with its fan-shaped fronds, also known as the "traveller's tree" as it conserves water in the folds of its leaves.

Mauritius is an island of flowers. They blossom everywhere, in the magnificent gardens of Pamplemousses, around the poorest huts and along the roadsides where the vermilion of coral-tree flowers, the gold of cassia and allamanda, the coppers and purples of flower-leafed bougainvillaea, oleanders, hibiscus and poinsettias blaze in the December heat. In graveyards, the perfect flower of the frangipani perfumes the memory of the deceased. Cress and pink pepper grow in roadside ditches, in cool streams trickling over moss. In wastelands, datura - the devil's flower - waves its little bells and delightful bushes of two-coloured lantana grow wild. In July the tall sugar cane with its pink feathery blooms lines the roads with walls of vegetation, against a background of blue, grey or mauve mountains and spanned, during brief moments of sun and rain, by brilliant rainbows.

Mauritius is an island of perfumes, a festival of fragrances sensed by sailors on the high seas miles before reaching land. The air is heavy with saffron and nutmeg, camphor and pepper. At harvest time the cane is burnt and at night an exquisite scent spreads from the blazing fields and mingles with the alcoholic aroma of the crushed stalks fermenting in the sugar refineries. In village markets the smell of dried fish is disguised by the emanations of onions, camphor (burnt to ward off evil spirits), and the Indian aphrodisiac cotomili.

Mauritius is an island of birds. The huge, vanished dodo may rest in peace. Yet even though some species are extinct, many still remain: woodcocks and hornbills, small Cape canaries and bulbuls, the cassava-bird which awakens the dawn, partridges, coots, sea-swallows and the martins that nest in the thatched roofs, more garrulous than the customers in the Prisunic supermarket at Curepipe.

*T*he beautiful house of Riche en Eau
near the east coast is listed as a historical monument. The house and estate are
the property of the Rochecouste family. The park is bordered by
the Rivière Créole.

*D*ue to their
isolation and environment,
some traditional houses still
bring to mind the closed
universe of the plantations,
the intimacy of family lives,
the verandah awaiting
evening visitors.

*T*he seven
waterfalls of Tamarind,
cascading as if down a
natural staircase of basalt
and lava, form as many
cool lakes. Many shades
of green here punctuated
by the Eau Bleue dam
(preceding pages) make up
this landscape typical of the
south-east of the island.

The ever-present sugar cane, proof of man's hard-working perseverance, assails the plateaux (above) or extends to the edge of the valleys its perfect chessboard, preserved from drought by powerful sprays (following pages).

*L*a Villebague was rebuilt
in the middle of the nineteenth century on the site
of the original building, which was erected in 1740 by
Athanase Ribretière de la Villebague. Villebague was a
native of Saint-Malo who, supported by Mahé de La
Bourdonnais, set up one of the first Mauritian sugar
refineries on the Piton. In modern times the house was
inhabited by the painter Gaëtan de Rosnay. Château
Trompette (above) dates from the 1870s.

*T*he proportions of the four-sided roof
and the verandah arcades combine perfect harmony with simplicity of line
at Béthanie, Beau-Bassin.

The Robillard Manor at Mahébourg houses the historical museum of Mauritius, in which cannon and cannon-balls recall the Battle of Grand Port.

*T*he Tour Blanche, near
Moka, was built by an English engineer in 1835. It became the property of the
Diocese of Port Louis and was subsequently inhabited by Benedictine monks
who named it "Mont Thabor". In the park a stream cascades through
luxurious vegetation.

*T*he *Réduit,
residence of the governor
general of Mauritius,
was originally a small
manor-house built by
Pierre Barthélémy David,
the French governor in
1748, to serve as a place
of refuge for women and
children if the English
attacked. It has come to be
called the "little Versailles"
of the tropics.*

*A*ll religious people have raised
sanctuaries to their gods, imposing or modest, chapels or cathedrals.
Mauritians of Indian origin are fervently attached to their temples, which
symbolise an ancestral culture.

*E*ven the simplest Tamil temple
represents the anchor of a religious feeling devotedly kept alive by
a community isolated in the heart of the plantations.

*T*he strange Montagne
du Corps de Garde, 718 metres tall, is situated near
Quatre Bornes. At its summit, the painter and poet
Malcolm de Chazal discerned the shape of a reclining
figure gazing towards the plains of the Rivière Noire.
The Tamil temple of Shri Siva Soopramaniar (above)
is perched on the mountain's slopes.

The Trois Mamelles and the Montagne du Rempart. The poet Malcolm de Chazal was fascinated by these peaks. He saw them as gods with their own cult.

*A*bout half the surface of the island
is suitable for farming, and sugar cane is grown on 92% of this land.
The agricultural workers in the fields call themselves "laboureurs"
(an old French term), while those who work in the sugar factories
are known as "artisans".

*D*ivided by farm tracks
and stretching to infinity, the sea of sugar cane waves
gently in the wind. The cane takes about twelve months
to reach maturity. By July, just before the harvest, the
young green shoots of December have grown into huge
walls of vegetation crowned by pinkish-beige plumes.
Above: The trucks that carry stones removed from the
land are loaded to the hilt.

This buffalo-drawn cart might be a picture from the past, yet this form of rural transport is still used along the grassy paths bordering the plantations, between canefields and squares of tobacco plants.

*W*omen do their washing in the island's
rivers and roadside canals, drying a palette of multi-coloured fabrics on the
banks. The waterlilies floating on this river are not only pretty - they're
edible, and are an ingredient in traditional Mauritian cooking.

*T*his marshy landscape in
the west of the island testifies to the initiative of Pierre
Poivre, who fostered the cultivation of a variety of
rice from Cochin China. Transport is by boat along
the canals, which furrow through the plantations like
blue veins on the patchwork of fields.

Seen from the air, the sugar-cane plantations resemble a green carpet with overlapping planes, its fanciful pattern formed by the winding paths and newly planted areas.

*I*ntroduced by the Dutch, the Java deer
is still prolific in Mauritius. Venison curry is one of the island's culinary
specialities, especially during the hunting season in June. About 3,000 deer are
shot every year to maintain a herd of 20,000, grazing mainly in the south-
west of the island. During droughts the deer are fed molasses and cane leaves
to prevent starvation and a consequent lack of venison.

*P*erched on a mountain, looking out towards the Rivière Noire and the Morne, Chamarel is one of the wildest and most beautiful spots on Mauritius. The Chamarel waterfall, known as the "Bride's Veil", cascades down a sheer drop of 90 metres into the Rivière du Cap. Damp and verdant, the surrounding forest is home to small monkeys, stags, wild boar and a multitude of birds.

A geological
phenomenon in the Rivière
Noire district: the multi-
coloured earth of Chamarel,
composed of volcanic ash
exposed by erosion. Amidst
the vegetation are curious
parallel tumuli, composed of
iron ore and mineral oxides
which are devoid of organic
matter and therefore prevent
anything from growing. The
earth is made up of at least
eight colours which never
mix together. This area is
one of the tourist attractions
of the island.

A sugar refinery amidst the cane.
Mauritius has about twenty such factories, which represent the final
industrial stage, after large numbers of workers have laboured in the fields.
In July when the cane is pounded the air is filled with a delicious scent.

The unusual light effects of dusk play on the cassava biscuit factory, just outside Mahébourg on the road to Grand Port. These biscuits, as unappetising in their dryness as the glutinous tapioca of our childhood, are nonetheless very popular on the island.

*T*he Morne
Brabant, an impressive
natural bastion like an
outpost on its peninsula, is
flanked on the left by the
Pointe Sud-Ouest and on the
right by the Pointe des
Pêcheurs and Pointe
Marron (following pages).

A lmost all the Mauritian coastline runs along a lagoon separated from the open sea by a coral reef. The reef is broken only where rivers flow into the sea, the fresh water prevent-ing coral from forming, and so providing fairways. Mauritius possesses nearly a hundred kilometres of beaches often shaded by filaos, a kind of hairy fir which makes the wind sing in its needles. Between Grand Gaube and Cap Malheureux in the far north, there are small islands on the horizon: Coin de Mire, Ile Plate and Gabriel islet.

The section of the coast going west via Pereybère, Grand Baie and Trou aux Biches houses the greatest number of seaside tourists on the island. Luxury or semi-luxury hotels, elegant weekend bungalows, holiday-club villages (including the Club Méditerranée at Pointe aux Canonniers), fashion and parasol boutiques make this is the Saint-Tropez of Mauritius with its yacht clubs, restaurants and night-clubs.

The west coast towards the south of Port Louis remains less developed; it has a more wild and natural magnificence. The sunsets there are sumptuous. Its climate is extremely hot, but it is exquisite during the winter months of June and July.

On the beach at Albion, in the bay of the Petite Rivière, one can still come across hidden fragments of Ming porcelain shattered in Pieter Both's shipwreck during the seventeenth century. A skindiving centre in the village of Flic-en-Flac offers visits to the admirable seabeds, abounding in fish, beyond the reef. At Tamarin, a small fishing village with salt marshes at the estuary of the river of the same name, there is a grey sandy beach ideal for surfers. This is the only beach on Mauritius with large breakers. The Rivière Noire, its shoreline edged with Eucalyptus forests, is an important centre for offshore fishing. This part of the coast going down towards the Morne, at the south-eastern tip, is breathtakingly beautiful.

The village of Souillac, in the south, is named after a French governor of the island (1799-1887). It also preserves the memory of the French poet Paul-Jean Toulet, a native of Pau but born to a rich Mauritian colonist from the Béarn and a Mauritian mother of Norman origin. Brought up in France after the death of his mother, Toulet discovered Mauritius at the age of twenty and stayed for two years in his father's house at Souillac. His travel diary gives a detailed description of life on the island at the end of the last century.

Souillac was also the home of the Mauritian poet Robert Edward Hart. He spent the last years of his life in a little house built of madrepore, which looked out onto the sea. Today it is a tiny and very moving museum. Hart is buried in the graveyard of Souillac, a dramatic coastal cemetery where, during cyclones, the sea covers the graves. People hardly ever bathe on this wild and beautiful coast, looking out over a savage expanse of water that stretches to the icebergs of the South Pole. But what beauty!

At the Pointe Desny near the bay of Mahébourg the sea is calmer. This seaside resort is favoured by the Mauritian bourgeoisie; wind-surfers and water-skiers are in their element here. Going towards Poste de Flacq, Poste La Fayette, Trou d'Eau Douce and Belle Mare, all types of water-sports can be practised. White sand alternates with black rocks on the beach at Roches Noires. On the east coast weekend resort bungalows stand next to big hotels like the Touessrock and the Saint-Géran.

This coast of Mauritius, swept by the south-east winds for ten months of the year, is ideal during the summer heat of December and January. While sunsets are the jewel of the west coast, exceptional moonrises illuminate the east.

*T*he majestic site of the Morne Brabant on the west coast evokes two historical events: the name of the huge block of basalt recalls the seventeenth-century Dutch colony, and the Passe de l'Ambulante facing it, the wreck of a royal ship in 1774.

*A*midst vegetation and mountains, the Rivière Noire salt marshes are like a giant mirror reflecting the colours of the sky or the brightness of the clouds. In the distance rises the Morne Brabant.

*T*he Tamarin salt beds. In the hot west-coast climate, the sea-water in the basins evaporates very quickly. At daybreak women dressed in blue and wearing rubber boots rake the brine.

*It was René Magon, governor of the
island from 1756 to 1759, who set up the first salt bed, run by the salt-traders
from Saintonge. The basins of the Tamarin salt bed are lined with basalt.
Their colours change from dawn to dusk according to the reflections of
the changing light of day.*

*F*ortier islet (above) is situated just off
the mainland, opposite the estuary of Petite Rivière Noire. Opposite: at the foot
of the Tourelle de Tamarin, the river of the same name flows into the sea.
The beach of grey sand is much frequented by surfers in July. A gap in the reef
creates large breakers on this beach, the only one on the island
where surfing is possible.

*T*he estuary of the Rivière
*Noire on the west coast. The flotilla on the right belongs
to a hotel with an offshore fishing centre reminiscent
of Hemingway's* The Old Man and the Sea.
*Catches include swordfish, tuna and bonito. Extended
jetties (above) allow one to reach the channel even
when the tide is at its lowest, thus linking the small
isles to the mainland.*

*O*n the west coast, with the Montagne
du Rempart on the horizon, Flic-en-Flac is a small fishing village where
witchcraft is said to be very much in practice. It is also a skin-diving centre.

*B*aie du Tombeau, a small roadstead north of Port Louis. It is named after the magnificent white marble tomb of an English governor of Bombay who died at sea in the eighteenth century and is buried here. The village, inhabited by civil servants, stretches along almost three kilometres of coast.

*T*he Hotel de la Pirogue is on the west coast. Built by a German architect, it takes its name from the shape of its roof, which resembles the underside of a dugout canoe or pirogue. It is run by a South African group that also owns the Touessrock and Saint-Géran hotels on the east coast. Excellent grilled fish is served in its restaurant on the beach.

*T*he dazzling beaches of the Hotel
Merville and the sheltered haven of Grand Baie with its lagoon,
excellent for water-sports as well as lazing in the sun.

*G*rand Gaube, on the north-east coast,
is both a lively seaside town and the scene of a September pilgrimage that
draws the faithful to its chapel dedicated to Saint Michael. Large numbers of
fishing-boats and pirogues are produced in the town's shipyards.

*T*he urban centre of Grand Baie in the north-west of the island opens on to one of the coast's finest natural havens. For this reason, no doubt, it is full of sailing enthusiasts and its crowning glory is the exclusive Yacht Club.

*F*ishing boats are moored within sight of Notre-Dame Auxilliaire at Cap Malheureux. The village is so named because it was here that the English put ashore when they invaded the island in 1810.

*T*he Baie de Bainbœuf, near Cap
Malheureux. Moored peacefully on the emerald lagoon with its white sand, the
fishing boats seem oblivious to the plane-loads of holiday-makers from around
the world who besiege the island weekly.

$M$are aux Lubines in the
lagoon of Saint-Géran. The Indian temple is built on
an islet linked to the mainland by a causeway.

*T*he north of Mauritius has no
mountains, and tourists flock to its white sandy beaches. Here, the bathing
amenities of the Trou aux Biches hotel.

The sand is white and the lagoon turns from blue to green at Belle Mare (east coast). There is a hotel here named after the wreck of the Saint-Géran on the reefs of the Ile d'Ambre in 1744. This shipwreck was the inspiration behind Bernadin de Saint-Pierre's novel Paul et Virginie. *In 1966, the Saint-Géran's bell was retrieved by divers; it is now in the Mahébourg museum.*

*P*arallel with the Pointe
Quatre Cocos, the promontory that houses the
Touessrock hotel enjoys the calm waters of the
Trou d'Eau Douce bay, on which nestles
the village of the same name.

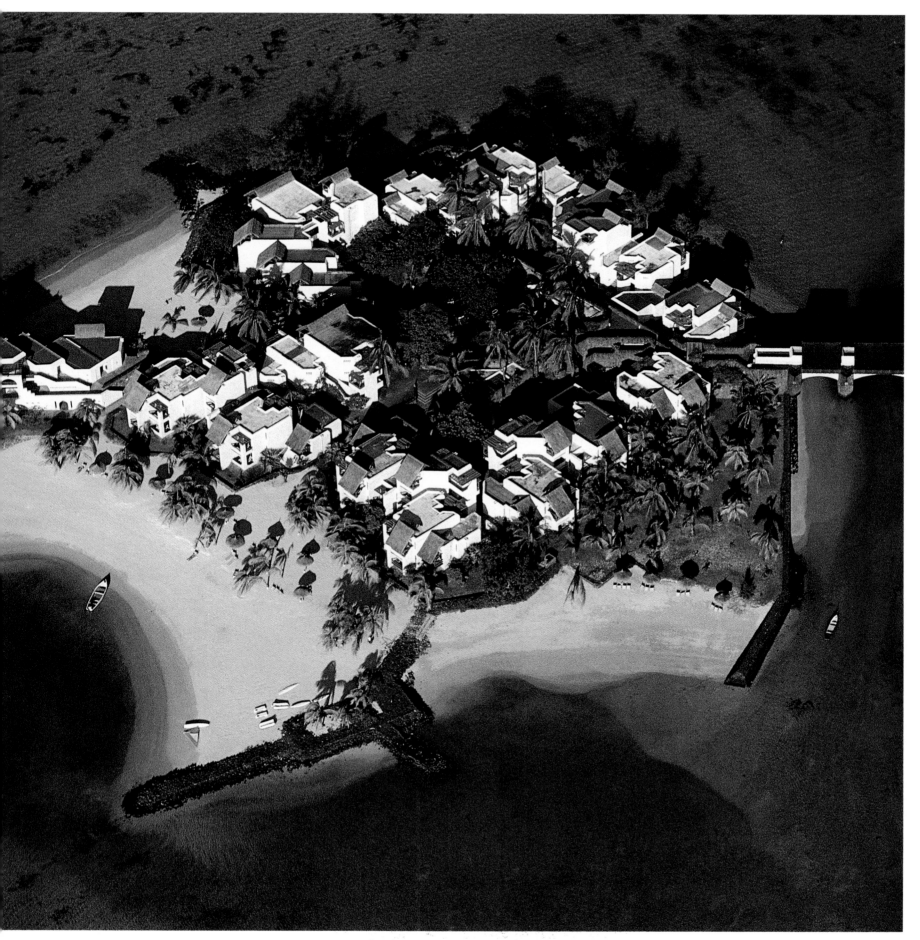

*T*he Trou d'Eau Douce
region offers sea-sports lovers transparent water
revealing luminous depths. The nearby Ile aux Cerfs,
covered with filaos, palms and jackfruit trees, is a
spot for walking and bathing after a fifteen-minute
crossing by speedboat. A narrow strait separates it
from the Ile de l'Est. On the large island the
Montagne du Chat can be seen.

*T*rawling in the lagoon. On Mauritius
the fish have amusing names, such as cobbler, fallen-lady and bastard.
In the shallows fishermen on foot stir the water with switches to direct
the fish into their nets.

129

*O*ver a sea-bed
that appears impressionistic,
through the limpid water
glides a boat that combines
the delicacy of a pirogue
and the robustness of a ship
on the high seas, evidence of
the know-how of Mauritian
naval carpenters.

*T*hree small islands off Mahébourg signal the approach of the east coast of Mauritius. On the Ile aux Fouquets, situated furthest out to sea, a now- disused lighthouse was built in 1864. A tax was levied on goods carried by ships entering the port, and served to maintain the lighthouses.

*S*eparated from Fouquets by Vacoas
(top left of photo above), the Ile de La Passe used to watch over the entrance
to the lagoon and the Mahébourg roadstead. The vestiges of the eighteenth-
century ramparts and artillery are still impressive.

*T*he private estate of Bel Air Saint-Félix is on the south coast. Its principal residence is on the mountain. This seaside house is a "campement", the Mauritian name for a seaside bungalow, typically with a thatched roof and used at holidays and weekends.

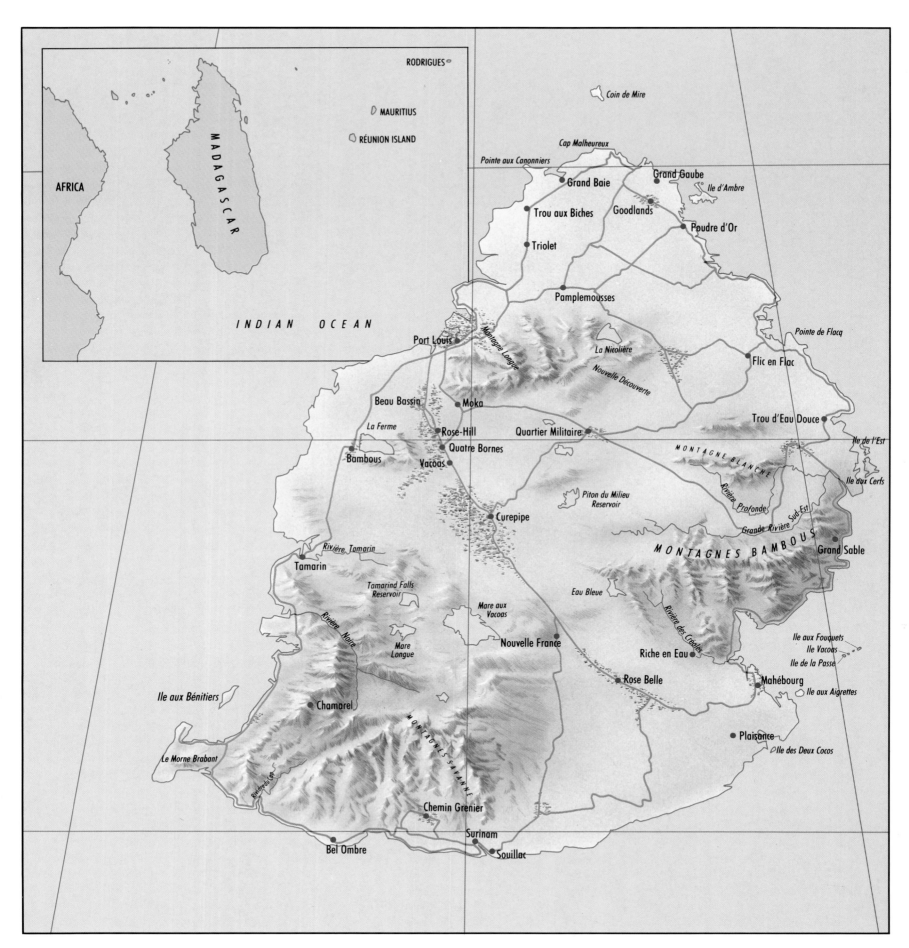

RODRIGUES

Coin de Mire

MAURITIUS

RÉUNION ISLAND

AFRICA

M A D A G A S C A R

Cap Malheureux

Pointe aux Canonniers

Grand Gaube

Grand Baie

Ile d'Ambre

Trou aux Biches

Goodlands

Poudre d'Or

Triolet

INDIAN OCEAN

Pamplemousses

Pointe de Flacq

Port Louis

Montagne Longue

La Nicolière

Flic en Flac

Nouvelle Découverte

Beau Bassin

Moka

Trou d'Eau Douce

La Ferme

Rose-Hill

Quartier Militaire

Ile de l'Est

MONTAGNE BLANCHE

Quatre Bornes

Ile aux Cerfs

Bambous

Vacoas

Rivière Profonde

Piton du Milieu
Reservoir

Curepipe

Grande Rivière Sud-Est

MONTAGNES BAMBOUS

Grand Sable

Rivière Tamarin

Tamarind Falls
Reservoir

Eau Bleue

Tamarin

Rivière Noire

Mare aux
Vacoas

Ile aux Fouquets
Ile Vacoas

Mare
Longue

Nouvelle France

Rivière des Créoles

Riche en Eau

Ile de la Passe

Ile aux Bénitiers

Mahébourg

Rose Belle

Ile aux Aigrettes

Chamarel

Plaisance

Le Morne Brabant

MONTAGNES SAVANNE

Ile des Deux Cocos

Rivière du Sud

Chemin Grenier

Surinam

Bel Ombre

Souillac

FURTHER READING

BERNADIN DE SAINT-PIERRE, JACQUES-HENRI *Conseil à un Jeune Colon de l'Ile de France*, 1818

BERNARDIN DE SAINT-PIERRE, JACQUES-HENRI *Paul et Virginie*, ed. Pierre Trahard, Garnier, 1977

BERNADIN DE SAINT-PIERRE, JACQUES-HENRI *Voyage à l'Ile de France*, 1773

CHARLES LE CENE, MICHEL *Voyages Célèbres et remarquables du Seigneur Jean Albert de Mandelsco*, Amsterdam, 1627

CONRAD, JOSEPH *Smile of Fortune* translated by G. Jean-Aubry as *Un Sourire de la Fortune* in *Oeuvres*, volume III, La Pleiade, 1987

DESVAUX DE MARIGNY, ISABELLE, VALENTIN LAGESSE, HENRIETTE *Living in Mauritius: Traditional Architecture of Mauritius*, photographs by Christian Vaisse, preface by Geneviève Dormann, Thames and Hudson, 1990

DORMANN, GENEVIEVE *Le Bal du Dodo*, Albin Michel, 1989

DUMAS JACQUES *Fortune de Mer à l'Ile Maurice*, Atlas Films

ROUILLARD, GUY *Histoire des Domaines Sucriers de L'Ile Maurice*, 1964-1979, The General Printing & Stationary Company Ltd, Mauritius

ROUILLARD, GUY *Le Jardin des Pamplemousses, Ile Maurice: Histoire et Botanique, 1729-1979*, The General Printing & Stationary Company Ltd, Mauritius, 1983

TOULET, PAUL-JEAN *Journal de Voyages* in *Oeuvres Complètes*, Laffont (collection bouquins), 1986

TOUSSAINT, AUGUSTE *Histoire des Iles de Mascareignes*, Berger-Levrault

TOUSSAINT, AUGUSTE *L'Océan Indien au XVIIème siècle*, Flammarion, 1974

TOUSSAINT, AUGUSTE *Port Louis, Deux Siècles d'Histoires 1735-1935*, La Typographie Moderne, Port Louis, 1935

TOUSSAINT, AUGUSTE *Une Cité Tropicale: Port Louis de l'Ile Maurice*, Presses Universitaires de France, 1966